Vacation Sex Quiz Book

Having accumulated a bunch of vacation time, Lea and Leo decide to spend the money they have saved by working overtime and head for a six-week vacation in the sun.

Their goal is a combination of sea, sex, and sun. However, figuring that making love in the sun never stopped anyone from learning a thing or two at the same time, they also decide to get a little deeper into the history, anatomy, mythology, and art of the whole sex thing.

The result is this quiz-cum-exercise book, based on their adventures and explorations, which offers a refresher course in eroticism and sexuality.

Whether you are lying on the beach in delightful company or squeezed under the canopy of a tent while the mosquitoes buzz around outside, forget your usual Sudokus, crossword puzzles, and Scrabble sessions, and enjoy these games and exercises, designed to enhance your sexual knowledge (and maybe curiosity).

Grab your pencils…

Having arrived at their vacation destination, Lea and Leo are lazing around naked on the beach...

They look at, discover, and describe each other...

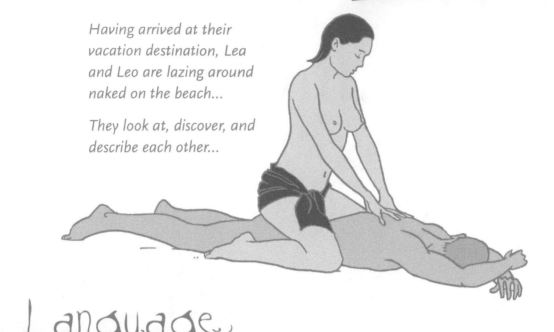

Language
Literature/Vocabulary

Read the following passages carefully and imagine the scenes involved. They are extracts from the novel *The Butcher* (Le Seuil, 1988) that the author, Alina Reyes, opted to write in a very neutral style, without using an erotic vocabulary or sophisticated metaphors.

1   *Then I climbed right on top of him, pressed my vulva against his genitals, and rubbed it up against his scrotum and his penis; I guided it with my hand to get it to penetrate me, and it was like a great flash of lightning, the dazzling arrival of the Savior, the instant return to grace.*

2   *I raised my knees, wrapped my legs around him, and rode him vigorously. Each time when, right at the top of the stroke, I saw his penis, all red and shiny, come out, I took it back in, trying to get it to penetrate me even deeper.*

3   *I was going too fast. He calmed me down gently; I unwrapped my legs and I sat on him. I remained motionless for a moment, contracting my vaginal muscles around his member.*

4 *He rolled on top of me and took his turn at riding me, supporting himself on his hands to avoid crushing me. His scrotum rubbed against my buttocks, and upon entering my vagina, his hard penis filled me, slipping and sliding on my deep vaginal walls, and while my nails dug into his buttocks, he breathed harder...*

5 *We came together, for a long time, our fluids mixing, our groans intermingled, coming right from the back of the throat, from the depths of our lungs, sounds completely unconnected to the human voice.*

F̲ill in the gaps and change the style of the language.　　　　**Levels of Language**

Using Street Language and Slang

1 Then I climbed right on top of him, pressed my .... against his ...., and rubbed it up against his .... and his ....; I guided it with my hand to get it to penetrate me, and it was like a ...., the dazzling arrival of the Savior, the instant return to grace.

2 He rolled on top of me and took his turn at riding me, supporting himself on his hands to avoid crushing me. His .... rubbed against my ...., and upon entering my ...., his hard .... filled me, slipping and sliding on my vaginal walls, and while my nails dug into his ...., he breathed harder....

Using a Poetic and Metaphorical Vocabulary

1 Then I climbed right on top of him, pressed my .... against his ...., and rubbed it up against his .... and his ....; I guided it with my hand to get it to penetrate me, and it was like ...., the dazzling arrival of the Savior, the instant return to grace.

2 He rolled on top of me and took his turn at riding me, supporting himself on his hands to avoid crushing me. His .... rubbed against my ...., and upon entering my ...., his hard .... filled me, slipping and sliding on my vaginal walls, and while my nails dug into his ...., he breathed harder....

5

There are so many words that refer to the male and female genitalia, or to the anus, when they are sources of pleasure, that it is difficult to keep track of them all.

Draw a line connecting the slang terms below to their actual meanings

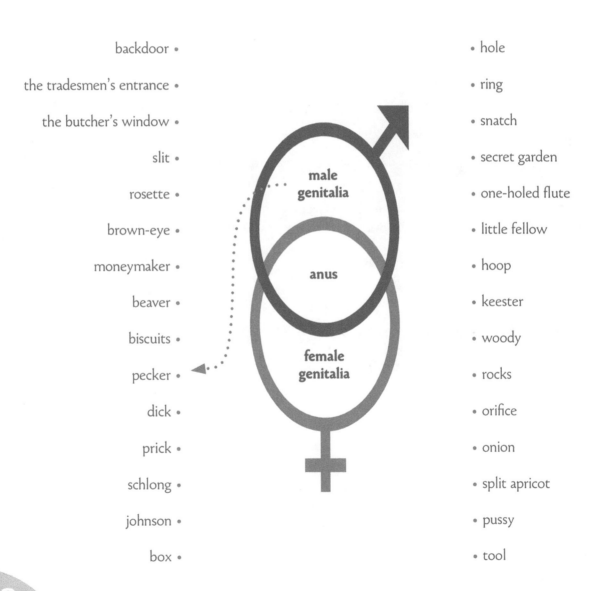

backdoor •

the tradesmen's entrance •

the butcher's window •

slit •

rosette •

brown-eye •

moneymaker •

beaver •

biscuits •

pecker •

dick •

prick •

schlong •

johnson •

box •

• hole

• ring

• snatch

• secret garden

• one-holed flute

• little fellow

• hoop

• keester

• woody

• rocks

• orifice

• onion

• split apricot

• pussy

• tool

Lea's and Leo's bodies conceal many mysteries: Do you know the proper names of the various parts of their sexual organs?

Draw a line from the name of the part to its location

penis

bladder

prostate

glans

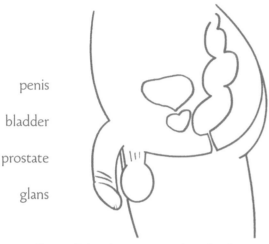

rectum

testicles

anus

urinary meatus

Guys: *Color the parts you love having caressed in pink, then quickly show the drawing to your partner.*

Female Sexual Anatomy

Draw a line between the name of the part and its location

ovaries

uterus

rectum

anus

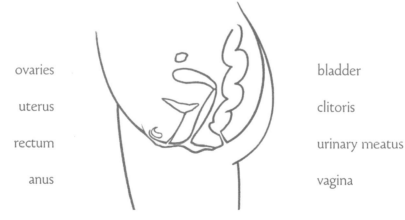

bladder

clitoris

urinary meatus

vagina

Ladies: *Color the parts you love having caressed in pink, then quickly show the drawing to your partner.*

History
Stories about Breasts

Various major figures in history, show business, and the fashion industry became famous (among other things) due to something special about their breasts.

Draw a line between the names of the well-known women below and the reason why their breasts are famous...

Lily Allen **1**

Sheyla Hershey **2**

Jayne Mansfeld **3**

Marilyn Monroe **4**

Janet Jackson **5**

Annette Funicello **6**

Anna Nicole Smith **7**

Marie Antoinette **8**

Madonna **9**

Pamela Anderson **10**

Sarah Bernhardt **11**

Diana Ross **12**

Jean Harlow **13**

A She has a piercing on one nipple—and how it got there was probably *not* a malfunction.

B This British singer has three nipples—and has bared them all in public. For extra credit, name the *Friends* character who had one too (three, we mean).

C As her movie career faded, she staged public "boob slips" that were caught on camera and gained publicity for her remarkably ample breasts.

D Molds were made of her breasts to make cups. Unfortunately, nobody thought to use the molds as cake pans.

E She wore some of the most memorable bras of the 1980s and '90s, including one that completely exposed her breasts.

F She got breast implants, enlarged them multiple times, had them removed when she stopped running on the beach, and later had them put back in again!

G She couldn't resist jiggling Lil' Kim's nearly naked breast during an MTV awards show.

H She would rub her nipples (we don't know if she called them "It") with ice before press conferences.

I She made her name by posing topless for a calendar—and was on the first cover of *Playboy* magazine. And then she made her name again—and again—and again....

J One of the great actresses of all time, she sometimes slept in a coffin to connect with tragic roles and was photographed bare-breasted, with her face half-concealed by a fan.

K She holds the Guinness World Record for largest silicone breasts at a size 38 KKK.

L She moved on from *The Mickey Mouse Club* to become one of the most popular 1960s beach babes.

M She made her fortune by placing her two large breasts on top of an old man's head.

*F*rom memory, describe your (or her) breasts using the following lists of words (that are usually used in medicine, art, or literature to describe anatomical features) and then compare your description to reality.

For example: For Leo, Lea's breasts are small and conical, their areolas are very dark with voluminous, cylindrical nipples. Lea thinks that they are large and pear-shaped, with pink areolas and small, somewhat spherical nipples!

General appearance
Pert, well-rounded, wide apart, slightly saggy, asymmetrical, etc.

Size
Ample, large, medium-sized, small, flat, etc.

Shape
Round, pear-shaped, fairly flat, pointy, spherical, conical, etc.

Color of the areolas
Dark (almost brown), red, pink, light pink, darker-colored around the edges, etc.

Areolas
Prominent, very large, large, circular, slightly oval, next to none, etc.

Nipples
Cylindrical and ample, taking up the whole width of the areolas, semi-spherical, flat, inverted, darker than the areola, etc.

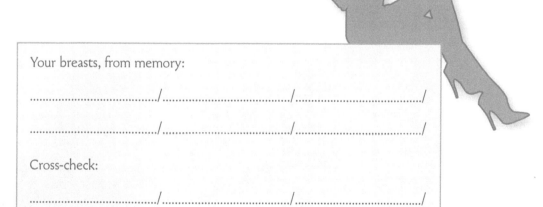

Your breasts, from memory:

............................./................................./................................/
............................./................................./................................/

Cross-check:

............................./................................./................................/
............................./................................./................................/

9

Language
Vocabulary

Breasts and nipples have always inspired novelists and poets.

Fill in the missing words in the following quotes, bearing in mind that in some cases the words involved include some strange comparisons.

egg / roses / fawns / thimbles / strawberry / bats / grapes

1 "A .... shows, half drown'd in cream" (Robert Herrick)

2 "Your two breasts are like two ...., twins of a gazelle" (*Song of Solomon*)

3 "Plump breast, whiter than an ...." (Clément Marot)

4 "A girl with nipples / like pink ...." (e. e. cummings)

5 "Her swung breasts / Sway like full blown yellow Gloire de Dijon ...." (D. H. Lawrence)

6 "Her belly and breasts, the .... of my vine" (Charles Baudelaire)

7 "the breasts hanging like two ...." (Anne Sexton)

Science
The Anatomy of the Breast

Do you know the right names for the various anatomical parts of the breast?

areola

nipple

Morgagni's tubercles

milk ducts

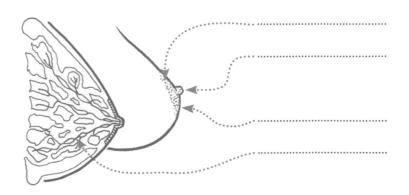

Art and History

Here are sketches (drawn from memory by our artist) of some famous bare breasts from art history. Match up each image with the correct name of the work and its artist.

1/.....

2/.....

3/.....

4/.....

5/.....

6/.....

7/.....

8/.....

A Picasso,
Reclining Sculptor

B Ingres,
The Turkish Bath

C Manet,
Olympia

D Fontainebleau School,
Portrait of Gabrielle D'Estrées and Her Sister

E Klimt,
Danae

F Modigliani,
Reclining Nude on a White Cushion

G Goya,
Maya Nude

H Balthus,
Nude with Cat

What's Napoleon Got to Do with It?

If his girl also wants to, there is nothing more delightful for a guy than making love between her breasts. But what do you call this sexual practice, which involves sliding an erect penis between a pair of breasts squeezed together to make them look and feel like a nice piece of ass?

Here is a list of expressions; identify the imposters:
Some of them refer to something altogether different.

1 French fuck   2 Napoleon on the ramparts   3 the lazy lady   4 Bombay roll

5 pearl necklace   6 on top of Old Smokey   7 titty fuck

Math
Mental Arithmetic

For greater comfort, calculate the cup size for your breasts (or your partner's breasts). To determine the right match for the breasts you are checking out, measure the diameter of the rib cage just under the bust. Add 5 inches to this measurement. Then measure the bust girth. The difference between this measurement and the previous measurement is what determines the cup size.

- If the difference is less than 0.5 inches: no cup size
- If the difference is 0.5 – 1.5 inches: cup size A
- If the difference is 1.6 – 2.5 inches: cup size B
- If the difference is 2.6 – 3.5 inches: cup size C
- If the difference is 3.6 – 4.5 inches: cup size D
- If the difference is 4.6 – 5 inches: cup size DD

Answer as quickly as possible! What is the cup size of a young woman who has

1 A rib cage diameter of 32.5 in. and a bust girth of 39 in.: ....

2 A rib cage diameter of 31 in. and a bust girth of 41 in.: ....

3 A rib cage diameter of 27 in. and a bust girth of 33 in.: ....

4 A rib cage diameter of 29 in. and a bust girth of 36 in.: ....

5 A rib cage diameter of 37 in. and a bust girth of 46 in.: ....

6 A rib cage diameter of 27 in. and a bust girth of 27 in.: ....

The Kama Sutra on Vacation

While staying at a seaside village, Leo and Lea discover a fun pastime: making love in a new position every time. Help them to find the best ones.

Language
Assume the Position

What sexual positions do the following mysterious names refer to? Is it a position involving:

A Standing   B Woman on man

C Man on woman   D On the side?

1 The strictly ballroom ....

2 The multitasking executive ....

3 Spooning ....

4 The chimney sweep ....

5 The hedge trimmer ....

6 The trophy wife ....

7 The milkman cometh ....

8 The mighty wind ....

9 The dragonfly ....

10 The pink flamingo ....

The dramatic lives of great lovers are an inexhaustible source of inspiration for cinema and are portrayed regularly on the silver screen.

1 *Read the following descriptions of famous figures portrayed in films and name the actor or actress who played the role.*

2 *While you are at it, for each great lover, state the name of the film in which they are portrayed (and, if you are a real moviegoer, provide the name of the director and the year in which the film was released)!*

A Roman Emperor Caligula was well known for his sexual excesses. This film shows him and his court in orgies and numerous sexual acts, and was the most expensive pornographic film ever made.

1. Who played Caligula? ....

2. In which film? ....

B John Wilmot, the 2nd Earl of Rochester, was a poet well-known for his debauchery and lewdness. He presented a poem to King Charles II called "Signor Dildo," which was one of many that got him banned from court.

1. Who played John Wilmot? ....

2. In which film? ....

C Cleopatra VII Philopator was the last pharaoh of Egypt and is famous for her liaisons with Julius Caesar and Marc Antony. The actors playing Cleopatra and Antony in this film had an affair during production and were later married.

1. Who played Cleopatra? ....

2. In which film? ....

D Franz Liszt can be called the "rock star" of classical piano; he had hundreds of fanatical female groupies and entertained multiple mistresses. This film uses more modern rock stars to portray his scandalous life on the road.

1. Who played Franz Liszt? ....

2. In which film? ....

E The reputation of the King of Israel reached the Queen of Sheba, and she traveled to meet him. In return, he gave her "all her desire, whatsoever she asked." In the film, the two are at first pitted against each other, but they end up in love.

1. Who plays the Queen of Sheba? ....

2. In which film? ....

F In a controversial portrait of the life of Jesus Christ, this film shows him unable to resist temptation, and he makes love to and fathers a child with the prostitute Mary Magdalene.

1. Who played Jesus? ....

2. In which film? ....

The lyrics in this dirty rap song use slang and vernacular English to describe the artist's sexual expertise. Rewrite the song, replacing the slang words with Standard English, or try to add your own dirty rhymes!

Language
Music/Vocabulary

I'm the nigga that the bitches have to watch like Swatch
When I'm up in their crotch I get stuck like stop
When I'm in their bed box I make them hop like scotch
They call me lego
Make them scream for blocks and blocks...
It's a small thang
How I do my thang
Never mind who I brang...
Like boomerang
We could get street like slang
Or I could eat you out
 till my lips is orange
  like Tang

I'm the .... that the .... have to ....

When I'm .... their .... I get ....

When I'm in their .... I make them ....

They call me ....

Make them ....

It's a small ....

How I do my ....

Never mind who I ....

Like boomerang

We could get ....

Or I could ....

till my ....

15

Try and guess what the activity described below was called in centuries gone by:

A An erotic manual from the eighteenth century defined a sex position as follows:

> *"The beautiful woman lay on a bench. The man stood, with his legs spread, astride the bench, happily rubbing his member in the soft valley formed by the two breasts which the woman's expert hands pushed as close together as possible."*

What was this position called?

.... Hussar style   .... Country-girl style

.... Sultan style   .... Bourguignon style

B From *Art de foutre en quarante manières* (Forty Ways to F*ck; 1790):

> *"The man having a fuck sat on a chair, while the girl hitched up her skirts and also sat down, although on his thighs and with her back turned to him; then she placed her hand under her dress, seized his erect tool, and inserted it, shafting herself under her own weight…"*

What was this position called?

.... The lazy lady   .... The shady lady

.... The mysterious woman   .... The dangerous woman

C *The Whores' Rhetoric* (1683) describes another position:

> *"When the man finds that the woman is the same height as he is, to see how skilful she is at that game, he makes her stand up, takes off her skirt and blouse, hugs her tightly, asks her to spread her thighs a little and, standing on his own two feet, does his business."*

What was this position called?

.... Taking the small lane .... Spending your time at ease

.... Crossing the dry river .... Passing through the narrow door

The words fuck, suck, buttfuck, and headfuck are
lacking in poetry and lyricism, to say the least.

*1n the list below, link each colorful or slang expression (on the left and
right) to the sexual practice (in the center column) it relates to.*

to go through •
the back door

• to pin her legs back

French job •

• to put the devil into hell

coitus

• to lunch at the Y

to park the •
pink Cadillac

• to play Ken and Barbie

to discover the •
mysteries of venus

• to play the trombone

fellatio

• burger munch

to gamahuche •

• cornholing

to go up the dirt road •

• head

to make mouth music •

cunnilingus

• Italian style

fudgepacking •

·········► • to eat seafood

doing the nasty •

• to go down the Hershey
highway

the teaspoon •

anal sex

blow job •

• to lay the lip

lollipop sucking •

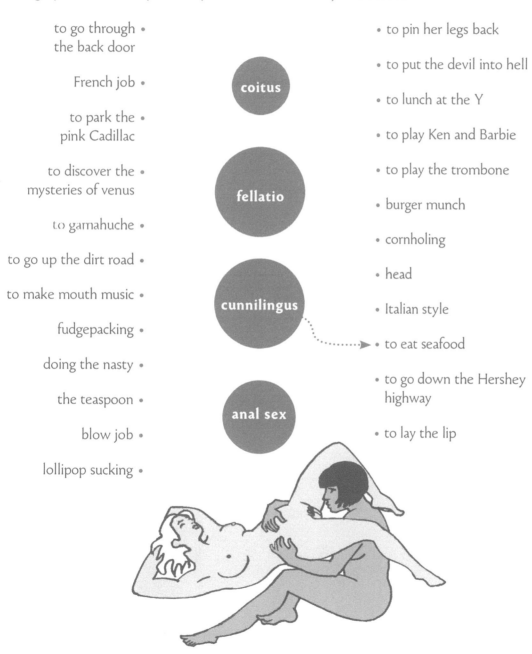

Lea, who is straddling Leo (see Figure 1),
would like to be done doggie-style (see Figure 5).

*Number the three intermediate figures in the order that will enable
Leo and Lea to change position without him having to pull out.*

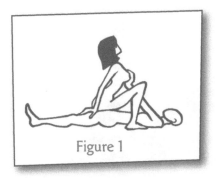

Figure 1

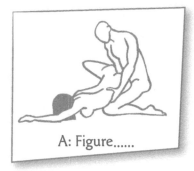

A: Figure......

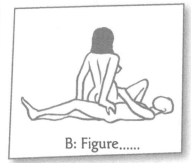

B: Figure......

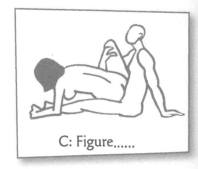

C: Figure......

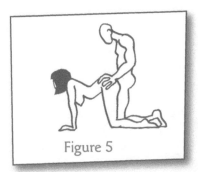

Figure 5

Erotic manuals often compare sexual positions to characteristics of animals, using zoological metaphors in order to refer to positions, from the simplest to the most sophisticated ones.

D raw a line between the description of the position or caress and its name:

The ostrich tail **1**

The congress of the sheep **2**

The camel's hump **3**

The spider's foot **4**

The swimming of the frogs **5**

The hare **6**

The tiger's approach **7**

The growth of the tortoise **8**

The congress of the cow **9**

Billygoat style **10**

A She is lying on her stomach with her legs spread, while he is on his knees behind her.

B She is on all fours while he is on his knees behind her.

C He is lying on his back, while she straddles him with her back turned to him and leans forward, moving frantically.

D She is on all fours, with her arms and legs stretched out, while he is behind her.

E She caresses his erect penis, just stroking it with the tips of her fingers.

F She lies on her side, with one leg up in the air, while he kneels between her legs.

G She lies on her back, with her legs folded up against her chest, while he lies on top of her.

H She stands and leans forward until her hands touch the floor, and he takes her from behind.

I She is on her knees, with her face toward the floor and her ass raised, while he is behind her.

J She lies on her back with her legs raised, while he stands on the end of the bed facing her.

Fun Time

C omplete the drawing, letting your imagination run wild...

History

Dirty Mythology

According to Greek and Latin literature, some of the great figures of antiquity and myth had complicated sex lives, and sometimes these people were associated with a particular incident or way of making love.

Match up the incidents that each of the following young ladies was the heroine of:

1 Andromache ....   **2** Cleopatra ....   **3** Leda ....

4 Venus ....   **5** Messalina ....

A A god disguised as a swan came down to earth in order to make love to her; in order to "receive" him, she laid on her back with her legs raised high in the air.

B Her favorite position for making love is well known; she straddled her husband, while in the adjoining room, guards watching them masturbated when hearing her come.

C Every night she left her palace in order to prostitute herself in her city's most sordid whorehouses.

D She was considered to be the greatest cock sucker of her time; some said that at one party she sucked off several dozen of her lover's friends.

E She cheated on her husband whenever he had his back turned, but one day he came up with a trap. He caught the cheating lovers in a strong, invisible net and called all the gods down to witness the sight.

Dirty Politics

Answer the following questions:

1 Marie Antoinette's lover was named…
.... Nielsen   .... Fersen   .... Hansen

2 Lady Godiva rode naked through the streets of Coventry, England, to protest…
.... The Church   .... Taxes   .... Clothing

3 The Bill Clinton scandal caused an uproar in 1998. According to Monica Lewinsky, how many alleged sexual encounters did the two have?
.... 21   3   9

4 Presidential candidate Gary Hart resigned from the 1988 race when he was photographed with a young woman on his lap who was not his wife. The name of the boat they were on was…
.... Sumfin Fishy   .... Nauti Lust   .... Monkey Business

5 One of the following French revolutionaries wrote pornographic novels. It was…
.... Danton   .... Robespierre   .... Mirabeau

For a heterosexual couple, lovemaking is an activity that, in most cases, is mainly limited to the following well-known acts or practices:

(a) vaginal coitus   (b) anal sex   (c) the man caresses the woman
(d) the woman caresses the man   (e) fellatio   (f) cunnilingus

*In the following questions, the **order** in which these acts are done is important in counting the combinations (for example, [a] followed by [b] and [b] followed by [a] counts as 2 combinations).*

1 To give themselves pleasure, how many different combinations can a couple employ that involve each of these six practices once?

....

....

....

2 How many possibilities can include 2 of these 6 practices?

....

....

....

3 For 2 given practices, how many possibilities are there? And for 3?

....

....

....

4 Based on that (and putting aside the previous order used so now [a] followed by [b] and [b] followed by [a] counts as 1 combination), how many combinations will involve 2 of the 6 practices? And 3?

....

....

....

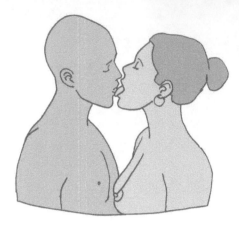

Making Love with Your Mouth

Lea and Leo's vacation in the sun is going wonderfully. Time passes as they kiss, caress, lick each other, etc. But being out in the fresh air makes them hungry, and our famished little couple are greedily devouring anything they can put in their mouths!

Language
Textual Analysis

In *Mes étapes amoureuses* (The Stages of My Love Life; 1890) Émile Desjardins extensively describes the sensual pleasure of a young lady with whom he has oral intercourse (to use the expression favored by sexologists). The clever author uses a metaphorical vocabulary to describe his girlfriend's genitalia and the pleasure it provides…

Rosy Lips

Scarcely had I placed my mouth on those two rosy lips than they opened up to my kiss, without any assistance from my fingers. A fine odor of violets was released from the slightly open gated haven, which proved to me that the sweet maid took care of her mouth down under just as well as the one up top.

Quickly my tongue penetrated the half-open gated haven and, right at the entrance, encountered a bold little prisoner who seemed to come to the tip of my lips, and on whom, in the center of these delights, I lavished sweet caresses. I did not have far to go before bringing about the sensual pleasure that caused pearls of love to come out of the pretty little mouth right in the center, at the same time as enchanted sighs were emitted from the mouth up top.

I moved away from the opening to contemplate my work; the little button, which was still quivering, was all shiny from light, white foam and the skin around the edge was clustered with pearls.

1 Identify the words or expressions that refer to female genitalia: ....
....

2 Identify the words or expressions that specifically refer to the clitoris: ....
....

3 The author compares his mistress's genitals to another part of her anatomy. Identify expressions or images that demonstrate this comparison: ....
....

There are numerous major authors in French literature who, at some time or other in their lives, produced an underground, pornographic work that was far different from their normally irreproachable prose.

Here is an account of a wild scene involving a threesome between a Romanian prince and two of his usual mistresses.

Mony, Culculine, and Alexine

The prince closed in with his member on Alexine's gaping cunt, which quivered in response to his approach:

'You are killing me!' she shouted. But his shaft penetrated up to his balls, then came out and went back in again like a piston. Culculine climbed onto the bed and placed her black pussy on Alexine's mouth, while Mony licked her asshole. Alexine wiggled her bum like a crazy woman, and placed a finger in Mony's ass, whose erection hardened even more as a result of this caress. He brought his hands back under the buttocks of Alexine, who clenched with an incredible force, gripping his enormous penis in her red-hot cunt so that it could scarcely move."

---

1 This text is an extract from *The Eleven Thousand Rods.* Who is its author?

A Vladimir Nabokov

B Leopold von Sacher-Masoch

C Guillaume Apollinaire

D Anaïs Nin

E Anne Desclos (or Pauline Réage, her pen name)

2 After you have answered question 1, write down which of the remaining four novelists wrote the following erotic works:

Venus in Furs: .... The Story of O: ....

Lolita .... The Delta of Venus: ....

Science

As the result of changing moral standards, certain sexual practices that were once considered to be perversions are now viewed as innocent pastimes…

1 In a 2002 report, how many people ages 25–44 claimed to have ever had oral sex with an opposite-sex partner?
.... A. 90% and 88%   .... B. 60% and 55%   .... C. 99% and 70%

2 According to *The Janus Report on Sexual Behavior*, what percentage of men and women reported a preference for oral sex to achieve orgasm?
.... A. 58% and 40%   .... B. 5% and 30%   .... C. 10% and 18%

3 How many men out of a thousand are well-endowed enough to fellate themselves to orgasm?
.... A. 30   .... B. 10   .... C. 3

General Culture

Fellatio in Antiquity

1 Fellatio is cited once in the Bible (Proverbs, Chapter 30, verses 18–20), but a rather mysterious way of saying it is used. What is it?
.... A. The way of a man with a maid
.... B. The foam of the sea on the lips of a maid
.... C. The mouth of a woman on the way of a man

2 Kabbalists say that one specific person in the Bible supposedly "invented" fellatio. Who?
.... A. Eve   .... B. Lilith   .... C. Judith

3 A queen from antiquity was nicknamed "big mouth" due to her talents when it came to fellatio. Was she:
.... A. Cleopatra   .... B. The Queen of Sheba   .... C. Esther

4 In Rome, a distinction was made regarding "active" fellatio, which is when the man performs an in-and-out movement in his partner's mouth. What was this practice called?
.... A. Pedication   .... B. Irrumation   .... C. Fornication

Look at the pictures below. Are Lea and Leo making love while watching themselves in a mirror? Not quite... Spot the seven differences in their reflection.

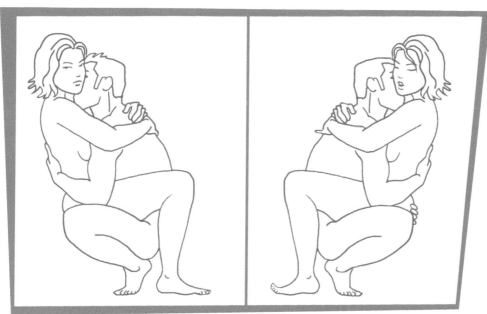

Word Origins

Many common words are derived from foreign ones that may have completely different (and sometimes surprising) meanings. Fill in the modern-day words next to their origin.

1 The name of this type of building comes from a Greek word that means to exercise naked, a common practice in ancient Greece. ....

2 The word .... comes from the Spanish word *aguacate*, which is derived from the Aztec word *ahuacati*, which means testicle.

3 The word .... comes from the Greek and means, "the writings of prostitutes."

4 The word .... comes from a Latin word meaning "vagina" because of the plant pod's similar appearance to the female genitalia.

5 It is very difficult to tell where the word "fuck" came from. Urban legend has it that in the Middle Ages it was an acronym for ....

Science

Glands

Is it because of the warm, humid conditions down below that there are so many of them? In any case, there are numerous glands in the vulva, and you should know where they are located...

1 Draw a line between the name of the gland and its location:

Skene's glands	**1**	**A**	On the labia majora
Sweat glands	**2**	**B**	On the labia minora
Bartholin's glands	**3**	**C**	Where the vulva and the vagina meet on the rear part of the labia majora
The sebaceous glands	**4**	**D**	Around the urethra or in the urethro-vaginal septum

2 Some of these in particular keep the vagina wet during sexual intercourse.

Which ones? ....

The "Ideal" Woman

According to the calculations carried out by one American beauty-products manufacturer, the "ideal" woman does exist! She is supposed to be 5'9" (69) inches tall, weigh 115 pounds, and her measurements are a bust measurement of 36 inches, a waist measurement of 24 inches, and a hips measurement of 36 inches...

Moreover, according to a survey disseminated in Japan, the measurements of the ideal woman could also be obtained based on height, which would determine all of her other measurements. In this case, the ideal woman's bust measurement would equal her height × 0.51; the waist measurement would equal her height × 0.37; and her hips measurement would be her height × 0.54.

Carrying out as few operations as possible, rounded to the nearest inch, calculate the "ideal" measurements for a woman whose height is:

A 5'11" (71 in.) .... / .... / ....

B 5'3" (63 in.) .... / .... / ....

C 5'8" (68 in.) .... / .... / ....

On the off chance (and adopting a tactful approach), check whether any of the women in your social circle have "ideal" characteristics...

The delicate art of fellatio regularly becomes the subject of raunchy anecdotes, in which the protagonists are some of the most beautiful woman of their epoch. Here are seven famous women from our times whose lives were affected by "fellatio stories."

Next to each woman's name below, write in the letter of the story associated with her.

1 Monica Lewinsky ....   2 Linda Lovelace ....   3 Chloë Sevigny ....

4 Paris Hilton ....   5 Maruschka Detmers ....   6 Britney Spears ....

7 Barbie Cummings ....

A A video, probably involving a lookalike, showed her going down on a man.

B Videos showing her sucking off one of her boyfriends nearly resulted in her going to prison, as the act was performed in a state where this practice is still illegal.

C An actress who made herself even more famous by giving her partner, Vincent Gallo, a blowjob (for real) in the film *Brown Bunny*.

D She was a White House intern who became world famous for sucking off the President and staining her blue dress with some Presidential sperm.

E This American porn starlet offered to go down on a policeman as payment for a speeding ticket.

F She was a porn actress who was the star of the film *Deep Throat* (directed by Gerard Damiano, 1973), and thereby won the much-coveted title of queen of fellatio.

G This actress performed fellatio in an Italian prison in a scene from the film *Devil in the Flesh* (by Marco Bellocchio, 1986).

Here are three extracts from texts describing "orogenital" sexual activities. In addition to the classic verbs "to lick" and "to suck," other expressions are used to describe the caresses performed...

Underline the expressions describing oral caresses.

1 *"The man lies on his back, the woman places herself on him so that her cunt is where his mouth is and his cock touches her mouth. Then the man places his tongue in her cunt and tickles her clitoris; she sucks his dick and caresses the foreskin with her tongue..."*
— Anonymous, *Art de foutre en quarante manières* (Forty Ways to F*ck), 1833

2 *"The charm of prostitute fingers purifying my penis, she has nice small breasts, and already her mouth is making itself familiar. Pleasant vulgarity, through your efforts the foreskin draws back, and this foreplay gives you childish contentment."*
— Louis Aragon, *Paris Peasant*, 1926

3 *"He licked me; he was the obstinate, determined type; he did it well; he moved his tongue gently over my clitoris; few men had done it to me so well. I was just surprised when he asked me to pull back my pubes and hold them with my hand so they would not get in the way of his tongue."*
— Christine Angot, *Rendez-vous*, Stock, 2006

Assign each extract (1, 2, and 3) to the sexual practice that it describes:

    A. Fellatio ....   **B.** Cunnilingus ....   **C.** 69 ....

Match the descriptions below to the texts:

    A. A prostitute and her client ....

    B. A couple at an orgy ....

    C. A young woman with an older lover ....

Rewrite paragraph 1 as if you were a naïve, inexperienced lover who is asking for these caresses.

....

....

....

....

....

Which of the following expressions refer to fellatio (A) and cunnilingus (B)?

1 Addressing the court ....

2 Speaking into the mic ....

3 Offering lip service ....

4 Giving a moustache ride ....

5 Giving a hummer ....

6 Pearl diving ....

7 Giving a knob job ....

8 Sipping the spring ....

9 Playing the flute ....

10 Donning the beard ....

At the beach, Leo finds Lea's buns extremely attractive and is highly tempted to give them a workout. Not wanting to rush things, he first searches through the classics of literature, cinema, and art for reasons to convince Lea to allow herself to be admired a little more closely.

Language
Literature/Vocabulary

A novelist who was a ballet dancer describes her encounter with a man who provided her initiation to anal sex (Toni Bentley, *The Surrender*, Regan Books, 2004):

1 *"He places me on my left side, pillows snug under my hip, raising my ass in a fetching little upward sideways arch. He grabs one of the tubes of K-Y scattered about the bed. I adore the sound as the top clicks open. Looking at me, he squeezes a gob onto two of his fingers. Looking to my ass, he spreads my cheeks so deliberately I cannot believe my luck. He rubs the gel gently, firmly onto my asshole, into my asshole, rimming the entryway, smoothing the passage."*

2 *"It's time.*
"Holding his cock, he guides it toward the crack in my ass, like a canoe aiming down a narrow ravine. I feel the smooth tip, both hard and velvety on my skin. The center of my asshole, like a magnet, gravitates toward the pressure. We meet. His key to my door, his positive to my negative, his plug to my socket."

3 *"And the light goes on.*
"Center to center, he nudges, I breathe, he pushes, I release, he pulses, I open, he pushes, I open, he plunges in, our eyes lock, and he sends me home."

1n this account, anal sex is accepted and even encouraged by the narrator. But an initial experience in this field may cause apprehensions. With changes to just a few words, the text could be transformed into an adventure that is not necessarily pleasant for the woman experiencing it. Change just a few words in the text to create a different version.

1 Looking to my ass, he spreads my cheeks so .... I cannot believe

  .... He rubs the gel ...., firmly onto my asshole, into my

  asshole, rimming the entryway, ...

2 Holding his cock, he guides it toward the crack in my ass, like .... I feel

  the smooth tip, both hard and .... on my skin. The center of my asshole,

  like a ...., ... the pressure.

3 Center to center, he nudges, I ...., he pushes, I ...., he pulses,

  I ...., he pushes, I ...., he plunges in, our eyes lock, and he

  ....

Metaphors and Comparisons

Toni Bentley describes her anus, her lover's penis, and the attraction she feels for anal sex by using a vocabulary and metaphors borrowed from the electrical sector.

Replace "magnet/we meet/his plug to my socket/positive/negative/and the light goes on/center to center" with words and expressions borrowed from another type of vocabulary without changing the meaning of the sentences.

For example: Maritime vocabulary. Delve into the vocabulary of the sea, the navy, sailing, and ports for metaphors that can be used to replace the vocabulary chosen by Toni Bentley.

....

....

....

....

....

31

general Culture

The Finest Museum Asses

Our artist sketched the finest asses in major art works on display in French museums. Do you recognize them?

1 Courbet, *Sleep*

2 Ingres, *The Valpinçon Bather*

3 Boucher, *The Blonde Odalisk*

4 Rubens, *The Three Graces*

5 Velasquez, *Venus at Her Mirror*

6 Man Ray, *Ingres' Violin*

7 Fragonard, *The Bathers*

8 Rodin, *The Kiss*

9 Cleomenes the Athenian, *Marcellus*

10 Renoir, *After Bathing*

A/......

B/......

C/......

D/......

E/......

F/......

G/......

H/......

I/......

J/......

On vacation, there is nothing better than total nudity.
But nudity also has its own history and stories.

*A*nswer the following questions:

1 Outside of naturist areas in France, women first appeared topless on the beach of…
.... **A.** Nice, in 1968 .... **B.** Cannes, in 1972 .... **C.** Le Pouliguen, in 1970

2 The first on-stage striptease show was in…
.... **A.** New York in 1917 on Broadway .... **B.** Paris in 1894 at the Divan Japonais
.... **C.** Berlin in 1912 on the location where *The Blue Angel* was later filmed

3 On Levant Island in France, when they were not on the beach, naturists used to have to wear a small g-string nicknamed the…
.... **A.** Minimum .... **B.** Thong .... **C.** Golden triangle

4 Naturists mock people in swimwear by calling them…
.... **A.** Frustrated .... **B.** Limeys .... **C.** Textiles

5 In the United States, a theatrical form of striptease is called…
.... **A.** Burlesque .... **B.** Grotesque .... **C.** Funny Stripping

6 During the 1960s, the first topless swimwear was called the…
.... **A.** Monokini .... **B.** Top Out .... **C.** No Limit

7 In a 2004 Roper poll, what percent of American adults said they'd gone skinny-dipping in mixed company at least once in their life?
.... **A.** 67% .... **B.** 13% .... **C.** 25%

8 He approved of nudist philosophy in one of his first books:
.... **A.** Dr. Seuss .... **B.** Walt Whitman .... **C.** Sir Arthur Conan Doyle

9 Naturists refer to nudists who shave their pubes as…
.... **A.** Free Willies .... **B.** Smoothies .... **C.** Brazilians

10 The first nude beach in the United States was established in 1967 in…
.... **A.** San Gregorio, California .... **B.** Puna, Hawaii .... **C.** Daytona, Florida

Science

1 *Circle the compound below that is not found in ejaculate...*
A. Vitamin C   **B.** Vitamin B-12   **C.** Calcium and magnesium
D. Phosphorus, potassium, zinc, fructose, and sorbitol   **E.** Proteins

2 *On average, a single ejaculation produces the following quantity of sperm:*
.... **A.** 2 to 5 milliliters   .... **B.** 6 to 10 milliliters   .... **C.** 10 to 15 milliliters

3 *Bearing in mind that the number varies considerably from one ejaculation to the next, what is the average number of spermatozoids per ejaculation?*
.... **A.** 400,000   .... **B.** 4 million   .... **C.** 40 million

History
Anal Sex Down Through the Ages

The attitudes of different civilizations and religions regarding anal sex have changed over the centuries. True or false?

1 According to Robert Van Gulik in his work *Sexual Life in Ancient China*, anal sex was an accepted, commonplace sexual act, but there was not supposed to be any ejaculation of sperm.   .... True   .... False

2 The *Kama Sutra* does not refer to anal sex, which was considered to be immoral by the ancient Hindus.   .... True   .... False

3 In Hell (as described in *The Koran*) no reference is made to people who practice anal sex.   .... True   .... False

4 In Ancient Greece, pederasty (an erotic relationship between an older man and an adolescent boy outside the family) was both natural and codified— the Erastes (adult lover) received the favors of the Eromenos (beloved adolescent).   .... True   .... False

5 In *The Art of Love*, Ovid advised against anal sex.   .... True   .... False

34

Lea and Leo are at a strange celebration: a costume party for nudists!

Can you find the seven differences between these two bizarre drawings?

To please Leo, Lea has decided to buy herself some skimpy, sexy lingerie, but she can't decide what to order, as she is confused about the names of the various items of lingerie that can optimally show off her fine breasts. Help her!

A a basque   **B** a bustier   **C** a corset   **D** a crop top   **E** body lingerie

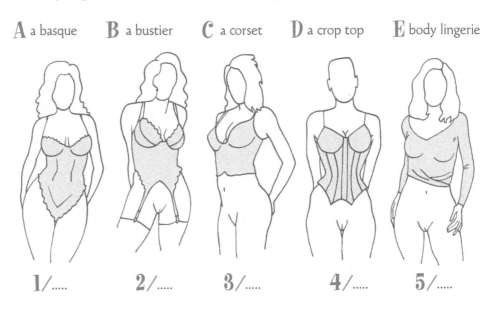

1/.....   2/.....   3/.....   4/.....   5/.....

Vocabulary

The word "bum" appears in numerous expressions and compound nouns. Find them based on the following definitions.

1 To hang out with no plan: ....

2 To ask for a (free) cigarette: ....

3 A young gay man who likes anal sex: ....

4 Taking a bath in a public sink: ....

5 Someone who hangs around the seaside: ....

6 A misleading suggestion: ....

7 A (British) tourist's money pouch: ....

8 Getting thrown out of a bar or restaurant: ....

9 A dead end street (think French): ....

10 An unjust sentence: ....

General Culture
Sex and the Cinema

Anal sex is not a theme that is common in "traditional" cinema. However, a few films have referred to it more or less directly. Fill in the sentences below using the names of the actors and the films in which anal sex is portrayed.

Who?
Molly Parker / Maria Schneider / Margo Stilley / PJ DeBoy

In which film?
The Center of the World / Last Tango in Paris / 9 Songs / Shortbus

1 A new boyfriend suggests to .... that they should spread butter on themself before he has anal sex with them in ....

2 In ...., ... and their lover decide to experiment with a third partner. As they are having anal sex, a stalker across the street videotapes them.

3 After a concert, ... has anal sex while traveling abroad in London. This film, ..., uses completely unsimulated sex scenes.

4 During a weekend of sex exploration, a man suggests a sex act called "fire and ice," involving alcohol, ice cubes, and anal sex to .... in ....

37

Draw a line between the name of each of the following callipygous (having a shapely rear end) ladies and the anecdote about her buns.

Brigitte Bardot **1**

Aphrodite **2**

Jennifer Lopez **3**

Beyoncé Knowles **4**

Sylvia Kristel **5**

Kim Kardashian **6**

Barbie **7**

The Callipygian Venus **8**

Catherine Bach **9**

Josephine Baker **10**

A She is depicted lifting her dress and exposing her well-proportioned, shapely buttocks.

B If she were real, her teeny-tiny legs would not be able to support the weight of her 40-inch behind!

C She prides herself on being "bootylicious."

D She hid her buns under a skirt made of fruit.

E She has one of the most well-known butts on reality television.

F A temple was dedicated to her, ... of the Beautiful Buttocks.

G Her large "assets" were rumored to be insured for a million dollars.

H She asked her lover, "Do you like my ass?" (in *Contempt*, one of her better-known movies)

I Her character popularized the short shorts known as "Daisy Dukes."

J She became famous by posing nude and showing off her bum on a couch.

Leo has offered Lea a new toy; a small vibrator that she always keeps in her beach bag. Vacations also provide a good opportunity for shopping, which can include going around to different sex shops to look for new sex aids.

Literature
Comparative Literature

Here is part of an erotically themed poem by Walt Whitman entitled, "I Sing the Body Electric":

Hair, bosom, hips, bend of legs, negligent falling hands, all diffused—mine too diffused;
Ebb stung by the flow, and flew stung by the ebb—love-flesh swelling and deliciously aching;
Limitless limpid jets of love hot and enormous, quivering jelly of love, white-blow and delirious juice;
Bridegroom night of love, working surely and softly into the prostrate dawn;
Undulating into the willing and yielding day,
Lost in the cleave of the clasping and sweet-flesh'd day.

Rewrite the poem using more modern sexual descriptions.
Be creative! Imagine the lovers are using toys or props in their adventure:

Hair, bosom, hips, bend of legs, ... hands, all ....;

Ebb stung by the flow, and flow stung by the ebb—love-flesh ....

and deliciously ....;

Limitless ....and enormous, quivering ....,

and delirious ....;

.... of love, working .... into the .... dawn;

.... into the willing and yielding day,

Lost in ....

Rubbers have an extensive history. Identify the right answers among the wrong ones below.

1 As an ancestor to the female condom, geishas used to use…

.... **A.** A folded lotus leaf, which lined the insides of their vaginas

.... **B.** A sheet of paper inserted into the back of their vaginas

.... **C.** Natural sponges

2 In the eighteenth century, to hold male condoms in place…

.... **A.** They were fitted with rubber rings.

.... **B.** They were fastened onto a sort of harness.

.... **C.** They featured fabric knots.

3 Condoms made using sheep intestines have been found dating back to…

.... **A.** 3000 bc in Egypt

.... **B.** 1000 ad in China

.... **C.** 50 bc in Rome

4 In Japan, condoms were once made using…

.... **A.** Lizard skin

.... **B.** Tortoise shell

.... **C.** Chicken skin

5 Having Italian soldiers who were susceptible to venereal diseases wear condoms was encouraged in Italy by…

.... **A.** Leonardo da Vinci

.... **B.** Gabrielle Fallope

.... **C.** The Borgia Pope

6 In France, advertising for condoms only became legal in…

.... **A.** 1968
.... **B.** 1981
.... **C.** 1987

7 "Condom" is also the name of a French village. The word "condom" is used in English because…

.... **A.** They were made in Condom from ancient times onward.
.... **B.** The inventor of the modern condom was born there.
.... **C.** For no reason—there is no connection.

8 The name of the main female condom currently used is…

.... **A.** Femotex
.... **B.** Femidon
.... **C.** Feminex

9 As condoms made from intestines could not stretch, to calibrate them, the Parisian stores selling them used to employ…

.... **A.** Prostitutes who knew most of the men in the city and their "measurements"
.... **B.** Streetwise young ladies who offered test rides
.... **C.** Very intuitive girls who could "guess these things"

10 With the help of her husband, this activist illegally imported large quantities of female condoms from Germany and the Netherlands in the early 1900s and helped boost their U.S. popularity:

.... **A.** Gertrude Stein
.... **B.** Simone de Beauvoir
.... **C.** Margaret Sanger

general Culture

The slang used by young American women who are somewhat preoccupied with romance is full of expressions for referring to their short-term lovers. If you are familiar with the television series Sex and the City, *you will have no trouble answering the following questions:*

Spot the odd one out. One of these five expressions does not refer to a nonserious boyfriend—which one?

.... Boy toy   .... Lug   .... Déjà fuck

.... Arm candy   .... Tofu boyfriend

Can you match up the definition for each of the four remaining expressions?

A A lover who could become something slightly more than a good quick lay: ....

B A lover who, to your astonishment, you realize (afterwards!) you have already had sex with some years ago: ....

C A talented lover who is just for sex! ....

D A lover who you like to show off in public because he is so decorative— in addition to being an animal in bed: ....

1 According to the Museum of Sex in New York, the vibrator was originally used as a medicinal treatment for female…

.... A. Sexual deviancy   .... B. Hysteria   .... C. Incontinence

2 Merkins (the bottom half of burlesque costumes) were originally created as "pubic wigs" for fifteenth century prostitutes. The designs helped hide…

.... A. Unwanted hair   .... B. Birth marks and scars   .... C. Lice and syphilis

3 This famous dominatrix pin-up girl admitted that she never whipped anyone in her life.

.... A. Dita Von Teese   .... B. Bettie Page   .... C. Betty Grable

4 In 2004 a sex toy was introduced that does not require batteries. It is run by…

.... A. A USB port   .... B. Solar power   .... C. A rechargeable stand

5 As of 2009 the only U.S. state where you cannot purchase a sex toy is…

.... A. Texas   .... B. Kansas   .... C. Alabama

Fun Time

Connect the Dots

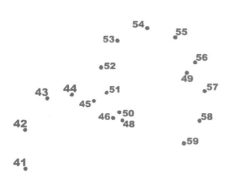

Connect dots 1 to 70 to find out what the mystery object is.

General Culture

Female fantasies regularly form the subject of reader surveys in women's magazines and in sexology reviews. According to the Kinsey Reports and The Great Sex Divide by Glen Wilson, what are the percentages of females who...

1 Use fantasy as a part of masturbation

...... **A.** 35% ...... **B.** 64% ...... **C.** 80%

2 Fantasize about romantic and exotic locations

...... **A.** 9% ...... **B.** 15% ...... **C.** 35%

3 Desire sexual acts with multiple people at once

...... **A.** 3% ...... **B.** 31% ...... **C.** 15%

4 Want to be dominated and role-play "forced" sex

...... **A.** 13% ...... **B.** 6% ...... **C.** 19%

5 Dream of making love with a stranger

...... **A.** 45% ...... **B.** 8% ...... **C.** 21%

Sex Toys in the Movies

Both male and female actors (some better known than others, admittedly) have played roles in films or soap operas (of a nonpornographic nature) that required their characters to use sex toys.

In the list below, write down the letter representing the erotic toy most favored by the character they played and then name the film in which the classic scene involving the actor and the sex toy occurred.

A Collar and leash   **B** Penis pump   **C** Remote-control vibrator

D Handcuffs   **E** An inflatable   **F** Glow-in-the-dark condom   **G** Sexy Rabbit vibrator

1 Kristin Davis: .... /..

2 Mike Myers: .... /..

3 Ryan Gosling: .... /..

4 John Ritter: .... /..

5 José Garcia: .... /..

6 Florence Guérin: .... /..

7 Vincent Elbaz: .... /..

Science

Animals have inspired the sex toy designers to create some amusing objects. Circle the name of the animal below that has not inspired a type of vibrator.

1 duck ....   2 rabbit ....   3 boar ....

4 doe ....   5 butterfly ....

Which Is Which?

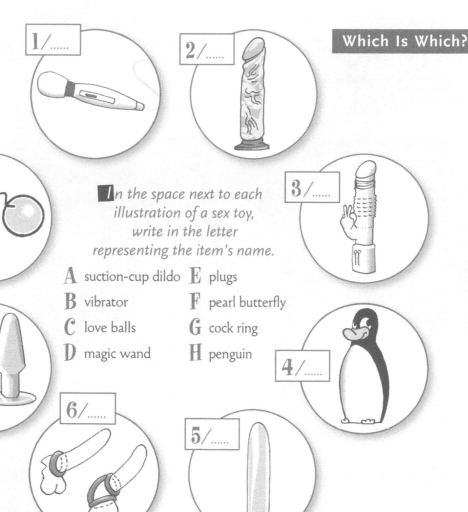

1/ ......

2/ ......

8/ ......

3/ ......

In the space next to each illustration of a sex toy, write in the letter representing the item's name.

A suction-cup dildo   E plugs
B vibrator   F pearl butterfly
C love balls   G cock ring
D magic wand   H penguin

7/ ......

4/ ......

6/ ......

5/ ......

45

Week 6

Erotic Fantasies

Lea and Leo's vacation is quietly coming to an end. They seem to have exhausted all of the sexual practices featured in the sex manuals and the magazines they have read on the beach. To spice up their final lovemaking, all that remains to be explored is the world of the "bizarre"…

Language
Textual Analysis

Here are three contemporary women's descriptions of multipartner sexual relations:

A Vanessa Duriès, from *The Ties That Bind* (Magic Carpet Books, 2005)

   "The men approached me and I suddenly felt dozens of fingers feeling me, penetrating me, frisking me, and dilating me.… I felt an intoxicating pleasure at being exhibited this way in front of strangers.…"

B Anna Rozen, from *Plaisir d'offrir, joie de reçevoir* (The Pleasure of Giving, the Joy of Receiving; Le Dilettante, 1999)

   "A penis in one hand, and with my other hand pressing the hollow curve of a nervous groin. The slightly timid softness of the tender dark-haired man who just replaced the determined energy of the blond-haired man with the Parisian accent. Every part of me is occupied, and no sooner does one let go than another one takes his place. Busy hands, mouth in a state of wonder.…"

C Catherine Millet, from *The Sexual Life of Catherine M.* (Grove, 2003)

   "They rammed me up against a perpendicular wall. Two men held me up under the arms and legs, while the others took it in turns hammering against the pelvis to which my whole person had been reduced."

Questions:

1 These three scenes are of different types: Write in the number of the descriptive extract above that matches up with the name of the extreme sexuality practice listed below:

a. threesome: ....   **b.** gang bang: ....   **c.** gang bang and exhibitionism: ....

2 None of these texts explicitly mention the women's sexual organs. Circle the words used to refer to them.

3 (a) Which words and expressions are used that compare these sexual activities to a simulation of aggression that is freely consented to? (b) What type of building are the authors' bodies implicitly compared to? (c) Make a list of the words that match the vocabulary specific to this type of architecture.

a. ....

b. ....

c. ....

The Vocabulary of Extreme Sex

Of course, you have no intention of subjecting yourself to the worst depravities, but it never hurts to learn about them.

For each of the terms below, choose the definition that provides its correct meaning:

1 A Roman night
- .... **A.** A swingers' term referring to one woman and dozens of men
- .... **B.** A swingers' term referring to one man and dozens of women
- .... **C.** An orgy, with a large number of partners of both sexes

2 A facial
- .... **A.** Ejaculating on your partner's face
- .... **B.** Fellatio
- .... **C.** Making love "face-to-face"

3 A glory hole
- .... **A.** A swingers nightclub
- .... **B.** An opening in a wall or partition that you stick your penis into so it can be sucked by someone on the other side
- .... **C.** A two-way mirror so you can watch sexual activities taking place in an adjoining room

47

4 A paddle

.... **A.** A wading pool for groups of people to make love in

.... **B.** The act of having sex in a wading pool

.... **C.** A type of leather fly swat that is ideal for spankings

5 The rowboat

.... **A.** An erotic position enabling a woman sitting on her lover's penis to caress two other kneeling men sitting on either side of her

.... **B.** Doing it in a rowboat

.... **C.** A variation on the missionary position

6 A daisy chain

.... **A.** Refers to a girl making love to several partners in succession

.... **B.** A type of tattoo worn as a recognition symbol by devotées of group sex

.... **C.** A sort of erotic chain consisting of partners who are licking or being licked, or sucking or being sucked…

7 A quickie

.... **A.** A quick fuck

.... **B.** Premature ejaculation

.... **C.** Gay slang for someone who changes partners in quick succession

8 A Prince Albert

.... **A.** A sexual position that is a variation of doggie-style

.... **B.** A penis piercing

.... **C.** A fetish costume

9 A double dong

.... **A.** A dildo with "two ends" that enables two people to penetrate themselves using it simultaneously

.... **B.** A threesome position in which the woman is sandwiched between two men

.... **C.** The act of fellating two men alternately

10 A fling

.... **A.** A brief sexual relationship

.... **B.** A metal dildo

.... **C.** Sex involving Scottish dancing

Our friends Lea and Leo have been invited to a debauched party in a chic apartment. It is particularly hot that evening, and soon most of the guests have stripped off their clothes and are between the sheets of an enormous red-satin canopy bed. Lea and Leo are exercising restraint, but there are some hotties in the house.

In addition to our two friends, there are:

A   Adeline, a bisexual girl

B   Bruce, a homosexual guy

C   Chantal, a heterosexual girl

D   David, a bisexual guy

E   Elvira, a heterosexual girl who does not do anal sex

F   Frank, a heterosexual guy, and

G   Gail, a girl who is up for anything.

Practical questions? (Give names as well)

1   How many partners can Frank hope to make love with?

  ....

2   How many partners could David hope to have anal sex with?

  ....

3   How many people are likely to want to lick Adeline while they suck Frank?

  ....

4   Bruce is getting bored all by himself, so David offers to suck him. To round things off, how many people can David suck if Frank decides to loosen up a bit?

  ....

5   Adeline wants to be part of a threesome. How many threesomes can she form part of?

  ....

  ....

General Culture

It goes without saying that many great men have been known for unusual sexual behaviors! Here are a few examples from history and literature.

Draw a line between the name of the man and the description of his erotic peculiarity.

Edward VII, King of England **1**

Immanuel Kant, the philosopher **2**

Guy de Maupassant **3**

Félix Faure, President of France **4**

Attila the Hun **5**

Marquis de Sade **6**

Louis XVI **7**

Adolphe Thiers **8**

Gandhi **9**

Victor Noir **10**

A He was capable of getting an erection on command.

B He slept among young, naked women at night to test his vow of chastity.

C He died on his wedding night.

D He was wanted for locking prostitutes in his castle and for giving some of them poisonous aphrodisiacs.

E His marble penis has become a cult object.

F A malformed foreskin delayed the consummation of his marriage.

G He adored making love in a bathtub filled with wine.

H He died a virgin.

I He had a mother and her two daughters as his mistresses, one of whom became his wife.

J He frequented women in brothels several times a day.

France is a great country with many fine scenic attractions that you should always visit with a naughty frame of mind. Here's the proof:

1 The statue of the "Four assless ones" is to be found in…
.... **A.** Lyons, France; it depicts four nude women with only their busts visible
.... **B.** Montpellier, France; it depicts four nude men with their backs to the wall
.... **C.** Chambéry, France; it depicts four elephants without showing their rear ends

2 The Grand Tetons mountains, literally meaning "Big Tits," can be found in…
.... **A.** Louisiana   .... **B.** Colorado
.... **C.** Wyoming

3 A depiction of the Mona Lisa with bare breasts is to be found in the French museum in…
.... **A.** Saint-Germain-en-Laye   .... **B.** Écouen   .... **C.** Chantilly

4 The small town of Fucking had to make their road signs theft resistant due to tourists visiting it in the country of…
.... **A.** Austria   .... **B.** Germany   .... **C.** Sweden

5 The *original* Playboy Mansion, which had a Latin inscription above the door stating, "If you don't swing, don't ring," was located in…
.... **A.** Los Angeles, California   .... **B.** New York, New York   .... **C.** Chicago, Illinois

6 John F. Kennedy responded to Marilyn Monroe's sensual rendition of "Happy Birthday" by saying, "Thank you. I can now retire from politics after having had 'Happy Birthday' sung to me in such a sweet, wholesome way." This event took place at…
.... **A.** The White House   .... **B.** The Washington Monument
.... **C.** Madison Square Garden

7 The can-can dance was perfected at the Moulin Rouge, located in…
.... **A.** Toulouse, France   .... **B.** Paris, France   .... **C.** Moulins, France

8 Mary Magdalene, the fisherwoman who was Jesus's friend, sailed to France after his crucifixion and supposedly landed in…
.... **A.** Corsica   .... **B.** The Camargue   .... **C.** The Gulf of Saint-Tropez

The erotic novel *Les Jeux du plaisir et de la volupté* (Games of Pleasure and the Pleasures of the Flesh), first published in 1932, and written by "a woman of the world," portrays the sexual escapades of a young woman named Suzy. Here is her description of a hot adventure she had in the Bois de Boulogne:

1 *"An orgy, Nicole…, one evening in the woods! …where I played the part of the Nymph raped by two satyrs!"*
   "Oh, two! Together?"

2 *"Of course. One fucked me, while the other fucked me up the backside. I was in between them, suspended in the air, with my legs bent back to my shoulders. I was totally naked and well illuminated by two car headlamps aimed at our group. And my husband was delighted to offer this show featuring my double coupling to ten or so of his friends and a few distinguished foreigners. Then, all of a sudden, the police arrived. And now you can understand why this divorce—the divorce imposed by our two families—was conducted in a closed hearing."*

3 *"Yes, everything becomes clear now…. But tell me: Your two satyrs, they did it at the same time? Did you like it? Did it give you pleasure?"*
   "Did it ever! It was wildly pleasurable. You can just see the scene: Those two costumed men and me naked in between them with their penises up my backside and my pussy. Oh, how I came, my dear. Came! You've got no idea, and just imagine my luck, Nicole, an unprecedented piece of luck: coming just before the cops arrived. Oh, let me fuck you, dearie!"
   "And me…she cried out all of a sudden, in ecstasy. Me too, Suzy, I'm coming, I'm coming…."
                (original text republished in French by La Musardine, 2007)

1 *Rewrite paragraph 2 from "One fucked me" to "distinguished strangers" in the form of a description by the policeman responsible for writing a report of his intervention at the Bois de Boulogne.*

....

....

....

2 As legend would have it, this text was written by a "woman of the world" living in Paris in the 1930s. Indicate the terms that enable you to identify that she was of a particular social class and lived in a particular period of history.

....

....

....

3 The "tableau vivant" presented as a show by Suzy was entitled "Nymph raped by two satyrs" by its author; come up with some other titles that are either more vulgar or more poetic, whichever you prefer.

....

....

....

A paraphilia is a desire for deviant sexual conduct — a small perversion in other words!

A Few "Paraphilias"

Draw a line between the official name of the paraphilia and what it is that excites people who have it:

Altocalciphilia	1	A	Travel
Maiesiophilia	2	B	Tears
Podophilia	3	C	Authoritarian women
Viragophilia	4	D	Partners who are angels, demons, phantoms, monsters, etc.
Pygophilia	5	E	A clothed sexual partner
Dacryphilia	6	F	A male partner dressed as a girl
Endytophilia	7	G	Pregnant women
Gynemimetophilia	8	H	Buttocks
Hodophilia	9	I	Feet
Spectrophilia	10	J	High heels

History

The French Emperor Napoleon I had a sex life that was as unusual as his destiny. How much do you know about it?

1. Napoleon lost his virginity under known circumstances:
   .... **A.** With a lady friend of his mother's in Ajaccio
   .... **B.** With a prostitute from the Palais-Royal
   .... **C.** With the companion of his sister Pauline

2. When he married Josephine, what information did he falsify in the marriage register?
   .... **A.** He changed his age
   .... **B.** He changed Josephine's age
   .... **C.** He changed the first name of his future wife and renamed her Josephine

3. Napoleon had a famous actress as his mistress. What was her name?
   .... **A.** Mademoiselle Pierre
   .... **B.** Mademoiselle Jean
   .... **C.** Mademoiselle George

4. The autopsy carried out on Napoleon's body revealed what special physical characteristic?
   .... **A.** He had a small penis
   .... **B.** He only had one testicle
   .... **C.** He was circumcised

5. One of his mistresses found his method of making love so boring that, to shorten the ordeal, she would…
   .... **A.** Have herself called by a maid-servant pretending that her husband was arriving
   .... **B.** Move the hands of the clock in her bedroom forward
   .... **C.** Get her enormous dog to jump up on the bed

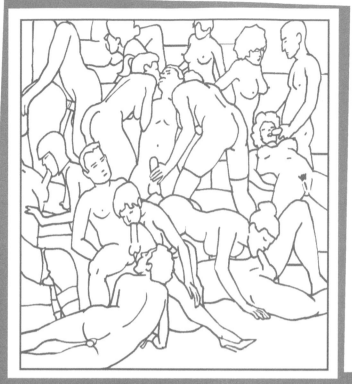

Leo and Lea are right in the middle of an orgy; spot the 7 differences in these intertwined bodies…

If they ever find their way out of here they might even make it home.

We hope you had a wonderful vacation too!

Answer Key

Week 1: Lovers' Bodies (pp. 4–12)

Language — Levels of Language (pp. 4–5)

Using Street Language and Slang

1. Then I climbed right onto him, pressed my pussy/cunt/slit against his dick/schlong/prick/Johnson, and rubbed it up against his balls/ball sack/nuts and his dick; I guided it with my hand to get it to penetrate me, and it was like a screaming orgasm, the dazzling arrival of the savior, the instant return to grace.

2. He rolled on top of me and took his turn at riding me, supporting himself on his hands to avoid crushing me. His swingers/balls rubbed against my ass/booty/backside, and upon entering my snatch/slit, his hard dick/prick/cock/wang filled me, slipping and sliding on my vaginal walls, and while my nails dug into his buns/cheeks, he breathed harder....

Using a Poetic and/or Metaphorical Vocabulary

1. Then I climbed right onto him, pressed my treasure trove/secret garden against his rod/clapper/joystick, and rubbed it up against his tackle/hairy chestnuts and his riot stick/baton; I guided it with my hand to get it to penetrate me, and it was like the rhythm of ecstasy/reaching seventh heaven/my own personal Xanadu, the dazzling arrival of the savior, the instant return to grace.

2. He rolled on top of me and took his turn at riding me, supporting himself on his hands to avoid crushing me. His family jewels rubbed against my haunches, and upon entering my scenic wonderland/my chamber of delights/rose/secret garden, his hard love wand/upstanding member/rock candy filled me, slipping and sliding on my vaginal walls, and while my nails dug into his trunk, he breathed harder....

Ways of Saying It (p. 6)

Female genitalia: split apricot, pussy, butcher's window, slit, snatch, secret garden, moneymaker, muff, box, beaver

Anus: backdoor, tradesmen's entrance, orifice, onion, rosette, hole, ring, hoop, keester, brown-eye

Male genitalia: pecker, prick, schlong, johnson, dick, tool, one-holed flute, little fellow, woody, rocks

Science — Male Sexual Anatomy (p. 7)

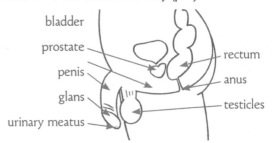

Science — Female Sexual Anatomy (p. 7)

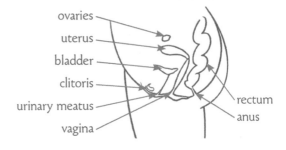

History — Stories about Breasts (p. 8)

1/B. Lily Allen; she showed it on English TV. Extra Credit: Chandler Bing had a "nubbin" removed on the television show *Friends*.

2/K. Sheyla Hershey of Brazil took the record in 2009 after nine surgeries and more than a gallon of silicone.

3/C. Jayne Mansfield

4/I. Marilyn Monroe

5/A. Janet Jackson; her piercing was revealed during the broadcast of a Super Bowl game.

6/L. Annette Funicello

7/M. Starlet and Playmate Anna Nicole Smith (1967–2007) supposedly seduced a billionaire by placing her ample breasts on his head.

8/D. Marie Antoinette left us moulds of her breasts; they were used to make cups and champagne glasses.

9/E. Madonna; her bra showing off her breasts was designed by Jean-Paul Gaultier.

10/F. Pamela Anderson

11/J. Sarah Bernhardt

12/G. Diana Ross did this during the 1999 MTV Video Music Awards.

13/H. Jean Harlow

Language — *Vocabulary (p. 10)*

1/strawberry 2/fawns 3/egg 4/thimbles
5/roses 6/grapes 7/bats

Science — *The Anatomy of the Breast (p. 10)*

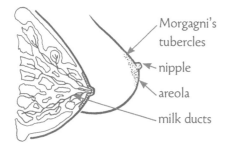

Morgagni's tubercles
nipple
areola
milk ducts

Art and History — *Famous Breasts (p. 11)*

1/E 2/H 3/A 4/C 5/B 6/G 7/F 8/D

What's Napoleon Got to Do with It? (p. 12)

1. Yes. This is a common expression for it.
2. Yes. This is an expression from the eighteenth century, as the engorged head of the penis looks vaguely like Napoleon's hat.
3. No. This is a sex position that does not involve much exertion.
4. Yes.
5. Yes, because when he comes, the guy leaves a pretty necklace around his girl's neck.
6. No. This is a straddling position.
7. Yes.

Math — *Mental Arithmetic (p. 12)*

1. $39 - (32.5 + 5) = 1.5$ in. cup
   (size B − 0.5 = a small size B)
2. $41 - (31 + 5) = 5$ in. cup (size DD)
3. $33 - (27 + 5) = 1$ in cup (size A)
4. $36 - (29 + 5) = 2$ in. cup (size B)
5. $46 - (37 + 5) = 4$ in. cup (size D)
6. $27 - (27 + 5) =$ flat-chested

Week 2: The Kama Sutra on Vacation (pp. 13–21)

Language — *Assume the Position (p. 13)*

1/A 2/C 3/D 4/B 5/C 6/B 7/C 8/B 9/B 10/A

History — *History, Cinema, and Great Lovers (pp. 14–15)*

A. 1: Malcom McDowell 2: *Caligula*, directed by Tinto Brass (1979)

B. 1: Johnny Depp 2: *The Libertine*/Laurence Dunmore (2004)

C. 1: Elizabeth Taylor 2: *Cleopatra*/Joseph L. Mankiewicz (1963)

D. 1: Roger Daltry 2: *Lisztomania*/Ken Russell (1975)

E. 1: Gina Lollobrigida 2: *Solomon and Sheba*/King Vidor (1959)

F. 1: Willem Dafoe 2: *The Last Temptation of Christ*/Martin Scorsese (1988)

Language—Music/Vocabulary (p. 15)

I'm the man that the ladies have to recognize
When I'm walking down their street I get
    hundreds of eyes
When I'm in their beds I make them squeal with
    delight
They call me the master of the night
Make them moan and groan…
It's a small operation
How I do my fornication
Never mind who I bring on vacation…
Like boomerang
We could get busy
Or I could work my magic till you're in a tizzy

The Language of Boudoirs (p. 16)

A. Country girl style
B. The mysterious woman
C. Crossing the dry river

Ways of Saying It (p. 17)

coitus: doing the nasty; to pin her legs back; to put
    the devil into hell; to play Ken and Barbie; to
    discover the mysteries of venus; to park the
    pink Cadillac.
fellatio: blow job; French job; lollipop sucking; to
    make mouth music; to play the trombone;
    head.
cunnilingus: to lunch at the Y; to *gamahuche* (from
    old French); to eat seafood; the teaspoon
    (an expression from the *Kama Sutra*); burger
    munch; to lay the lip.
anal sex: to go through the back door; to go down
    the Hershey highway; to go up the dirt road;
    fudgepacking; Italian style (the Italians say
    "French style"); cornholing.

Science—Spatial Geometry (p. 18)

A/Figure 4   B/Figure 2   C/Figure 3

Erotic Zoology (p. 19)

1/J   According to *The Perfumed Garden—
    A Manual of Arab Erotology* by Sheik
Nefzawi, an erotic work from the sixteenth
century that was somewhat of a hardcore
counterpart to *The Thousand & One Nights*.

2/B   According to *The Arab Breviary of Love*,
by Ahmed ibn Suleiman, a book written
in the sixteenth century at the request of
the bloodthirsty Sultan Selim I, who had
become impotent.

3/H   According to *The Perfumed Garden*.

4/E   Cited by Anaïs Nin in her erotic short
stories.

5/A   According to *Forty Ways to F*ck*
(anonymous, 1790).

6/C   According to *The Sublime Discourse of the
Candid Girl—Manual of Chinese Erotology*
(circa 1566).

7/I   Same source as for answer 6.

8/G   It is the "5th position" described by the
Candid Girl in the *Manual of Chinese
Erotology*.

9/D   According to the *Kama Sutra*.

10/F   According to *The Perfumed Garden*.

History—Dirty Mythology (p. 20)

1/B   She straddled her husband, Hector, and
moreover this position was called the
"Andromache."

2/D   Her reputation as an "expert cocksucker"
is doubtless the result of scandalmongering
by Caesar's enemies, who hated this exotic
mistress he had brought back from Egypt.
Nicknames for her were "big lips" and
"open mouth."

3/A   Zeus came to visit her disguised as a swan.
The position involving raised legs adopted
by Leda was named after her in ancient
times.

4/E   She and her lover, Mars, were trapped by
Vulcan, who called all of the gods to enjoy
the totally pornographic spectacle of these
two great beauties intertwined naked in a
steel net.

5/C   According to Juvenal, the wife of the

emperor Claudius devoted herself to the worst sorts of nocturnal debauchery, offering herself in Roman whorehouses to the first man who came along. Moreover, she was a bigamist. Oh well, never mind!

Dirty Politics (p. 20)

1/Fersen; he attempted in vain to organize her escape from various Parisian prisons
2/Taxes, which were imposed upon tenants by her husband
3/Nine, (though not all have been proven)
4/Monkey Business
5/Mirabeau, author of *The Raised Curtain*, among other publications

Math — Complex Combinations (p. 21)

1. For the 1st practice, there are 6 choices. The practices may only occur once, which then leaves 5 possible choices for the 2nd practice (which already makes 6 × 5 = 30 possibilities). Likewise, for choosing the 3rd practice, there are now only 4 possibilities remaining. And so on until the last practice is chosen. This gives 6 × 5 × 4 × 3 × 2 × 1, or 720 different possibilities.

2. The reasoning is similar to the reasoning for the previous question: 6 choices for the 1st practice and 5 for the 2nd practice, amounting to 30 possibilities.

3. For example. let's consider practices (a) and (b). The possibilities are as follows: (a, b) and (b, a). The answer is therefore 2.
   Now let's add a practice; (c) to keep things simple. There are 3 possibilities for the 1st position (a, b or c), and then a choice between the 2 remaining practices for the 2nd position and, lastly, only one remains for the 3rd position. Therefore the answer is 3 × 2 × 1 = 6 possibilities.

4. Now we have set aside the order used in the arrangements for the practices (the mathematical term used in this case is "combination"). So the number of combinations is the number of possible arrangements (cf. questions 1 and 2) divided by the number of possibilities (cf. question 3) so that we can do away with the order concept. Therefore, respectively, the answers are (6 × 5)/2 = 15 combinations and (6 × 5 × 4)/(3 × 2) = 20 combinations.

Week 3: Making Love with Your Mouth (pp. 22–29)

Language — Textual Analysis (p. 22)

1. Slightly open gated haven; mouth down under; half-open gated haven; center of these delights; pretty little mouth right in the center; opening
2. Little prisoner; little button
3. The author compares his girlfriend's genitals to a mouth (see answer 1); he continues the comparison by comparing the young lady's intimate odor to the odor of her breath (a fine odor of violets), and compares her vaginal secretions to a thin thread of saliva, the sort that caused an appetite or satedness (light, white foam). In addition to that, the young lady's labia are compared to rosy lips.

Pornographers (p. 23)

1/C
2. *Venus in Furs*/B   *The Story of O*/E   *Lolita*/A   *The Delta of Venus*/D

Science — Fellatio and Cunnilingus Down Through the Ages (p. 24)

1/A 2/C 3/C

General Culture — Fellatio in Antiquity (p. 24)

1/A.   Here is the full Biblical text:
"There be three things which are too
   wonderful for me,
Yea, four which I know not:
The way of an eagle in the air;

The way of a serpent upon a rock;
The way of a ship in the midst of the sea;
And the way of a man with a maid.
Such is the way of an adulterous woman;
She eateth, and wipeth her mouth,
And saith, I have done no wickedness."

2/B. According to the *Sexologia Lexicon*: "The erotic urges leading to fellatio are probably due to the mythical fantasy of Lilith whose vagina is linked to her mouth…" Because, according to the Kabbalah, our ancestor Lilith, Adam's first wife, had this strange characteristic…

3/A
4/B

Fun Time—Spot the Differences (p. 25)

Language—Word Origins (p. 25)

1/gymnasium   2/avocado   3/pornography
4/vanilla   5/Fornicate Under Command/Consent of the King

Science—Glands (p. 26)

1. 1/D   2/A   3/C   4/B
2. All four, but mainly the Skene's glands and the Bartholin's glands.

The "Ideal" Woman (p. 26)

A/5'11" (71 in.)—36/26/38
   71 in. × 0.51 = 36.21 or 36 in.
   71 in. × 0.37 = 26.27 or 26 in.
   71 in. × 0.54 = 38.34 or 38 in.
B/5'3" (63 in.)—32/23/34
   63 in. × 0.51 = 32.13 or 32 in.
   63 in. × 0.37 = 23.31 or 23 in.
   63 in. × 0.54 = 34.02 or 34 in.
C/5'8" (68 in.)—35/25/37
   68 in. × 0.51 = 34.68 or 35 in.
   68 in. × 0.37 = 25.16 or 25 in.
   68 in. × 0.54 = 36.72 or 37 in.

History—Fellatio Stories (p. 27)

1/D 2/F 3/C 4/B 5/G 6/A 7/E

Literature—"Oral" History (pp. 28–29)

1. "Tickles the clitoris"; "making itself familiar"; "moved his tongue."
2. A/2   B/3   C/1
3. A/2   B/1   C/3

Ways of Saying It (p. 29)

1/A 2/A 3/B 4/B 5/A 6/B 7/A 8/B 9/A 10/B

Week 4: The Back Is as Good as the Front (pp. 30–38)

Language—Literature/Vocabulary (p. 30)

1. Looking to my ass, he spreads my cheeks so brutally/savagely I cannot believe the pain. He rubs the gel violently, firmly onto my asshole, into my asshole, rimming the entryway, stretching my back passage roughly.
2. Holding his cock, he guides it toward the crack in my ass, like a ram breaching the gate of a citadel. I feel the smooth tip, both hard and rough on my skin. The center of my asshole, like a shell closing, revolted by the pressure.
3. Center to center, he nudges, I resist, he pushes, I clench, he pulses, I repel him, he pushes, I clench, he plunges in, our eyes lock, and he reams me all the way in.

Metaphors and Comparisons (p. 31)

magnet: abyss
we meet: he sinks into my ocean
his plug to my socket: his ship in my port
anode: port
cathode: starboard
and the light goes on: and the storm lifted
center to center: his wave crashing on my shore,
    etc.

General Culture — The Finest Museum Asses (p. 32)

1/C 2/H 3/E 4/B 5/F 6/I 7/A 8/G 9/J 10/D

Totally Naked (p. 33)

1/A 2/B 3/A 4/C 5/A 6/A 7/C 8/A 9/B 10/A

Science — About Sperm (p. 34)

1. Nothing to delete…sperm contains some of all
   of these
2/A, and even that's quite a lot…
3/C—and yes, that really is a lot!

History — Anal Sex Down Through the Ages (p. 34)

1. True
2. False; only sanitary recommendations are
   provided. Anal sex should follow vaginal
   penetration rather than being in the opposite
   order, which is just common sense!
3. False! The poor sodomites are among those
   who are treated the worst!
4. True
5. False. To the contrary, Ovid wrote that a woman
   must not forget "that she has two sexual
   organs."

If you find any errors in this
answer key, please e-mail us
at editorial@hunterhouse
.com. We're also looking for
new books in this series.

Fun Time — Spot the Differences (p. 35)

Language — Froufrou — Erotic Lingerie (p. 36)

1/E 2/A 3/B 4/C 5/D

Vocabulary (p. 36)

1. To bum around
2. To bum a smoke
3. Bumboy
4. Bum bath
5. Beach bum
6. A bum steer
7. Bumbag
8. Given the bum's rush
9. Cul de sac (from French, meaning literally
   "bum of a bag"!)
10. A bum rap

General Culture — Sex and the Cinema (p. 37)

1. Maria Schneider, *Last Tango in Paris* (Bernardo
   Bertolucci, 1972)
2. PJ DeBoy, *Shortbus* (John Cameron Mitchell,
   2006)
3. Margo Stilley, *9 Songs* (Michael Winterbottom,
   2004)
4. Molly Parker, *The Center of the World* (Wayne
   Wang, 2001)

Little Stories about Famous Rear Ends (p. 38)

1/H 2/F 3/G 4/C 5/J 6/E 7/B 8/A 9/I 10/D

Week 5: Toys (pp. 39–45)

*Literature — **Comparative Literature** (p. 39)*
Answers will vary.

*History — **The History of Condoms** (pp. 40–41)*
1/B
2/C (Casanova had pretty ones with pink knots)
3/A
4/B (Very young tortoises, with very fine shells, taken from the stomach…)
5/B (He was a famous anatomist)
6/C (Yes, as late as that)
7/C (It comes from the name of the doctor of King Charles VII who prescribed their use)
8/B
9/C (Like the famous salesgirls at the Gros Milan store in Paris in the eighteenth century)
10/C

*General Culture — **Sex and the City** (p. 42)*
1. Lug: An acronym for Lesbian Until Graduation, referring to the uncertain sexual status of young women who hit on their female classmates until they become graduates and then opt to become strictly heterosexual…
2. A. Tofu boyfriend   B. Déjà fuck
   C. Boy toy   D. Arm candy

Props and Toys (p. 43)
1/B 2/C 3/B 4/A 5/C

*Fun Time — **Connect the Dots** (p. 43)*

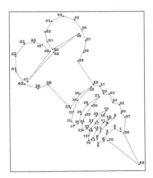

*General Culture — **Female Fantasies** (p. 44)*
1/B 2/B 3/C 4/A 5/B

Sex Toys in the Movies (p. 44)
1. G: Kristin Davis playing Charlotte York, one of the leading ladies in *Sex and the City*, uses a Sexy Rabbit vibrator.
2. B: Mike Myers playing the spy *Austin Powers* (directed by Jay Roach, 1997) who is a fan of the penis pump.
3. E: Ryan Gossling in the film *Lars and the Real Girl* (by Craig Gillespie, 2007) falls in love with a blow-up doll.
4. F: John Ritter, alias Zach Hutton, a character in the Blake Edwards film *Skin Deep* (1989), wears a fluorescent condom, just like the boyfriend of the woman he is sleeping with, resulting in a superb glow-in-the-dark parody of *Star Wars*, with the light sabers being replaced by fluorescent erect penises.
5. A: José Garcia, who is an S&M freak, drags his submissive partner along on a collar and leash in *Love Bites* by Antoine de Caunes (2001).
6. C: Florence Guérin comes when her lover Jean-Pierre Kalfon uses a remote-control vibrator in *Le Déclic* (Jean-Louis Richard, 1985), a film adapted from the comic strip by Manara.
7. D: Vincent Elbaz, or at least the character he plays, likes to make love with girls who are handcuffed in *Summer Things*, by Michel Blanc (2002).

*Science — **Zoology** (p. 45)*
3/boar. The duck inspired Duckie the vibrating duck, which looks like a bath toy, which won the prize for the Best Sex Toy of the Year at the 2003 Erotic Awards! Since it appeared in the series *Sex and the City*, the vibrating rabbit (the Sexy Rabbit or Jack Rabbit) has become the most famous and widely used sex toy. It is a multifunction vibrator that tickles everything

at the same time. The John Doe vibrator is a popular brand. The vibrating butterfly is a small massager that you press up against the clitoris.

Week 6: Erotic Fantasies (pp. 46–55)

Language — Textual Analysis (pp. 46–47)

1. a/B (threesome: three partners including two men)   b/C (gang bang: One woman with a large number of men)   c/A (gang bang and exhibitionism).
2. In me; every part of me; pelvis…
3. a: "suddenly," "penetrating me"…the author describes herself as the victim of a kind of sudden invasion of her body; b: "every part of me is occupied," the author compares her body to a besieged fortress; c: "They rammed me," "my whole person had been reduced," the author is immobilized and defeated. In all these cases, the vocabulary used relates to the siege of a fortress.

The Vocabulary of Extreme Sex (pp. 47–48)

1/C (B is merely a wonderful nightmare…)
2/A, in porno slang   3/B   4/C   5/A   6/C
7/A   8/B, Queen Victoria's husband had one; hence its name   9/A   10/A, even though it is not very poetic…

Math — Lea and Leo's Orgy (p. 49)

1/Four: Adeline, Chantal, Elvira, and Gail
2/Four: Adeline, Bruce, Chantal, and Gail
3/Two: David, Gail
4/Five: Adeline, Chantal, Elvira, Gail, and Frank
5/Six: Chantal and David/Chantal and Frank/ Chantal and Gail/David and Frank/David and Gail/Frank and Gail

General Culture — The Sexual Characteristics of Great Men (p. 50)

1/G   (He adored making love in a bathtub filled with champagne, particularly before he ascended to the throne, back when he used to do the rounds of all the Parisian bordellos.)

2/H

3/A   (He was able to get an erection on command and won bets doing so.)

4/J   (He died in 1899 at the Élysée (the Presidential Palace) while making love to his mistress, a woman of dubious reputation by the name of Marguerite Steinheil.)

5/C   (He died on his wedding night with Ildico, a Germanic blonde.)

6/D

7/F   (His malformed foreskin delayed consummation of his marriage with Marie Antoinette. A small operation fixed that, although only much later.)

8/I   (He had a mother and her two daughters as his mistresses. He married one of the daughters, Élise Dosne, in 1833.)

9/B

10/E   (A journalist who died in a duel — his statue's marble penis has become a cult location in the Père Lachaise cemetery in Paris, its recumbent figure showing off a promising protuberance in its crotch.)

Geography — Sexy Geography (p. 51)

1/C 2/C 3/C 4/A 5/C 6/C 7/B 8/B

Language — Orgy in the Bois de Boulogne (pp. 52–53)

1. Example of a rewrite: "The offending party, Madam Suzy X, was caught in the act, as naked as a jaybird, suspended in the air with her legs folded up to her shoulders by two

men in costumes indulging in contact of a sexual nature both genitally and anally, this constituting the actual offense of exhibitionism and public indecency, with these circumstances being aggravated by the presence of spectators—some of whom are suspected of being foreign nationals."

2. "Car headlamps," "distinguished foreigners," "costumed men," and, generally speaking, the staid erotic vocabulary: "satyrs," "penis," "pussy," etc.

3. Examples: "The meat in the sandwich"; "DP in the Bois de Boulogne" (DP standing for "double penetration"); "fucking in mid-air"; "the bird of pleasure on its perches"; etc.

Science—A Few "Paraphilias" (p. 53)

1/J 2/G 3/I 4/C 5/H 6/B 7/E 8/F 9/A 10/D

History—Napoleon I, the Emperor of Sex? (p. 54)

1/B. With a prostitute from the Palais-Royal, chosen because she herself had lost her virginity to a military man…

2/All three He made himself older, he made her younger, and he renamed her Josephine, feminizing her second Christian name (she was called Marie-Joseph-Rose)

3/C. Mademoiselle George, who was considered to have a "great temperament"

4/A. It seems he had a small penis, but it is impossible to verify this information as the organ has disappeared and was probably purchased by an American urologist

5/B

Fun Time—Spot the Differences (p. 55)

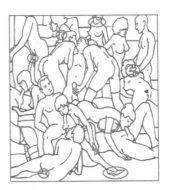

Other titles in the Dare… series

Dare… to Have Anal Sex by Coralie Trinh Thi

Dare… to Have Sex Everywhere but in Bed by Marc Dannam

Dare… to Try Bisexuality by Pierre des Esseintes

Dare… to Try Bondage by Axterdam

Dare… to Try Kama Sutra by Marc Dannam and Axterdam

— with more to come!
Follow us on Twitter (twitter.com/hhadults)
and Facebook (www.facebook.com/hunterhouse)